Step-by-Step
PYROGRAPHY

BOB NEILL

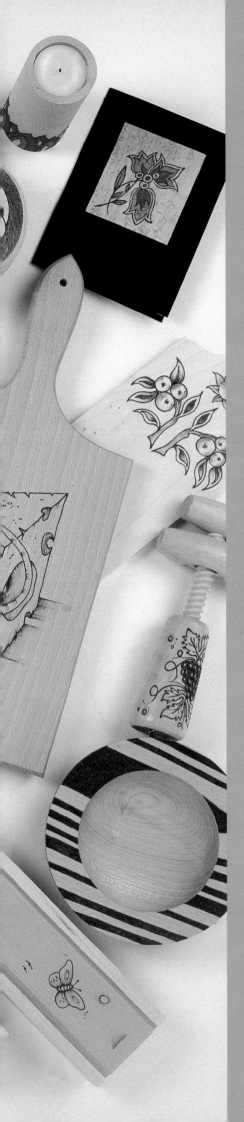

Step-by-Step
PYROGRAPHY

BOB NEILL

GUILD OF MASTER CRAFTSMAN PUBLICATIONS

First published 2005 by
Guild of Master Craftsman Publications Ltd
166 High Street, Lewes
East Sussex, BN7 1XU

ISBN 1 86108 491 9

British Cataloguing in Publication Data

A catalogue record of this book is available from the British Library.

Managing Editor: Gerrie Purcell
Production Manager: Hilary MacCullum
Photographer: Anthony Bailey
Editor: Alison Howard
Designer: Rebecca Mothersole

Colour reproduction by AltaImage
Printed and bound in Singapore by Kyodo Printing

CONTENTS

PROJECTS

ABOUT THE AUTHOR

Bob Neill has always been involved in art and craft. He studied at Cardiff College of Art, Birmingham University and Trent University, Nottingham. He lives in Derbyshire, but travels widely.

For more than twenty years, Bob taught art in London and Derbyshire, and helped to develop basic design ideas in art education. During the 1960s and 1970s his large abstract paintings, mosaics and metal constructions were exhibited in galleries across the country. He has designed and made toys for disabled children, and in 1975, he exchanged ideas with toy designers in the USA and Canada thanks to a Winston Churchill Travelling Scholarship.

By the late 1970s he had joined the pyrographic revival. His decorated turned work developed through his many contacts on the craft fair circuit and teaching at Craft Supplies. In 2002, he was awarded a Shackleton Trust Scholarship to teach pyrography in the Falklands.

He can be seen demonstrating at many of the major woodturning shows in the UK, Norway, Belgium, Germany and the USA.

INTRODUCTION

Pyrography is one of the oldest traditional crafts. It is the burning of designs on items, usually wooden, but it can also be used on leather, cork, fabric and paper.

Traditionally, pyrography was used to decorate domestic utensils such as bowls, spoons and drinking vessels. Early examples from many cultures can be seen in museums in London, Paris and other major cities. These artefacts include honey pots from Madagascar, a bamboo goblet from India, a wooden beer mug from Estonia, carved dolls from the Ivory Coast, and wooden boxes from Poland. During the Arts and Crafts Movement, pyrography was used to decorate large pieces of furniture, sometimes in the form of relief carving.

Basic equipment

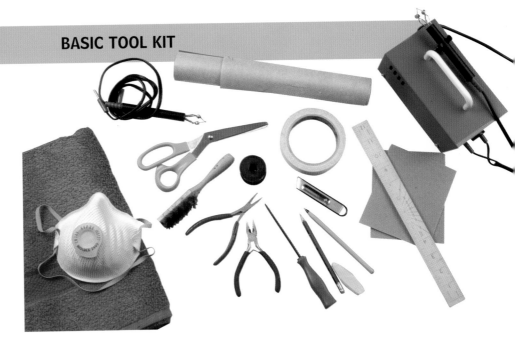

I have used most machines available, from soldering irons to the hot wire machine I now use (see list of suppliers, page 80). This is more expensive but is the choice of most professional pyrographers. Most people have well-stocked tool boxes but you may need to buy a few of the items below.

Control unit
This plugs into the mains and has a pilot light. The variable heat control knob produces a precise temperature.

Pen
This plugs into the unit and uses different tips. The spoon-point supplied is good for shading and calligraphy, and I make my own drawing nibs (see page 11).

Ruler
Use to create straight edges and map out patterns.

Carbon paper or transfer paper
Use with a hard, sharp pencil or ball-point pen to trace the outlines of your design.

Scissors
For cutting carbon/transfer paper, card and drawing paper

Soft wire/suede brush
This is useful for cleaning the wire nib of the pen. Sandpaper can also be used.

Eraser
Use this to remove pencil lines after the burning process.

Screwdriver
For changing wire nibs.

Pliers & flat-nosed pliers
For cutting the wire and shaping the nib.

Wire
Cut to size and use to form replacement nibs.

Masking tape
Use this to fix down carbon paper and drawings when transferring to the wood.

Pencil
B, 2B and HB pencils are useful for drawing designs.

Towel
Use a folded towel to raise the hand so bulky pieces are easier to work on.

Dust mask
Essential to protect agains inhalation of smoke.

Craft knife or pencil sharpener
Your pencil must be sharp for good, clear drawings.ful for planning designs.

Sandpaper
Use this to produce a good, smooth surface and to sand off small mistakes.

Extra equipment

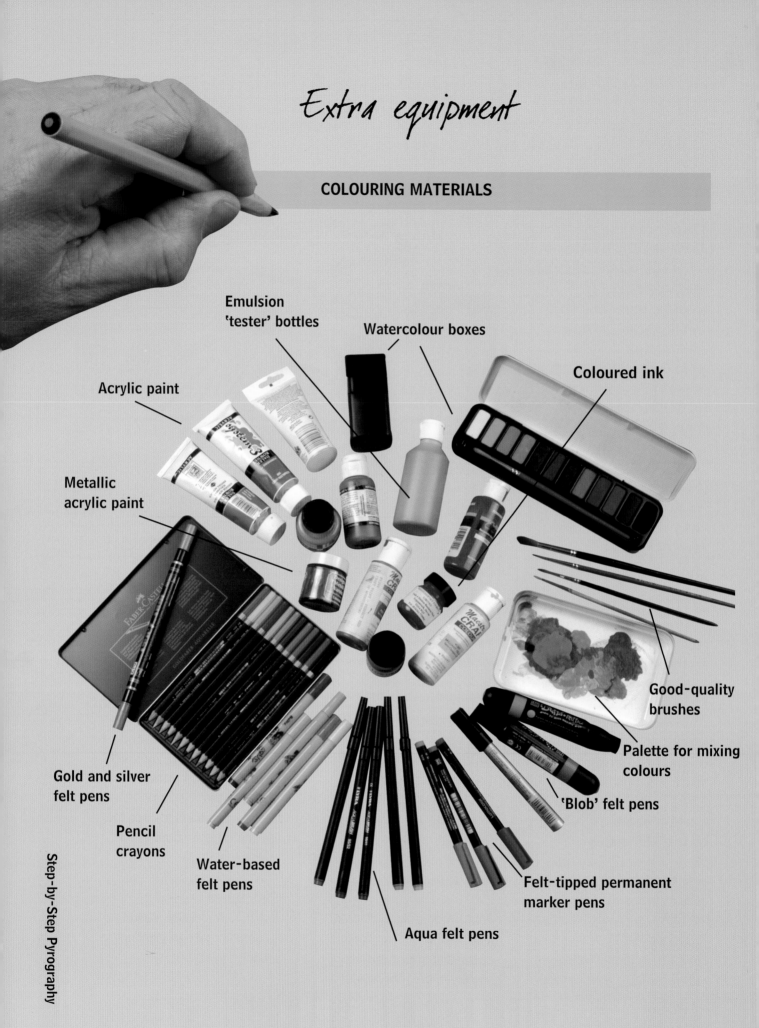

Emulsion 'tester' bottles

Watercolour boxes

Coloured ink

Acrylic paint

Metallic acrylic paint

Good-quality brushes

Palette for mixing colours

Gold and silver felt pens

'Blob' felt pens

Pencil crayons

Water-based felt pens

Felt-tipped permanent marker pens

Aqua felt pens

Choosing blanks

BLANKS

Blanks for pyrography are widely available. For just one item, try local hardware stores or the kitchen departments in major stores or supermarkets. Blanks are also available in bulk from specialist suppliers, which brings the price per item down considerably. You may have a friend who turns wood, which is how I obtain bowls and the needlecases featured on page 74.

Choosing different types of wood

From a distance, a pyrography design looks like a pencil drawing; close-up, it resembles an engraving. Line quality varies depending on the surface. On soft woods like pine, it tends to blur and run to create smoky areas. A line burnt on harder wood, such as sycamore, is cleaner and more exact. The woods used in this book are sycamore, beech and good-quality birch ply. Lime, holly and maple are also a good choice for pyrography, but soft woods tend to give an uneven line when burnt, and other types of wood may be too hard or too dark to produce a good effect.

On more unusual choices of material, including spalted beech or burr maple, being bold and adventurous can produce striking results.

Using templates

A wide variety of metal templates is available from specialist craft shops, and over the years I have built up quite a collection. Individual templates are reasonably priced, and they can be used again and again so they are good value.

You could punch out your own card shapes, or cut designs from thin card using a pair of scissors as well as using plastic stencils.

Rubber stamps

When selecting rubber stamps, choose ones with good raised outlines and no blocked-in areas. The easiest ones to use are those made from clear plastic so that you can position them exactly as required on your chosen surface.

Making nibs

Nibs are shaped from nickel chromium wire. There are four grades: 26 SWG (finest), 25 SWG, 24 SWG and 23 SWG (thickest). The best one to use is 25 SWG. For most work, the wire is pinched to a point. Experiment to produce a range of shapes.

1 Cut a piece of 25 SWG wire, about 3cm long.

2 Hold the wire between thumb and forefinger.

3 Bend into a U-shape.

4 Loosen the screws so the ends of the wire slide between the prongs and retaining grommets, then re-tighten.

5 Using pliers, pinch the loop to form a point.

6 The finished nib.

Spoon Points

Ready-made spoon points are available. They can also be made by twisting the U-shape so that you have a small circle at the tip. Hammer this out on a hard metal surface.

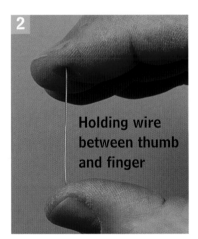

1 Cutting wire

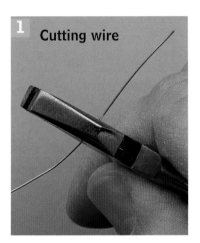

2 Holding wire between thumb and finger

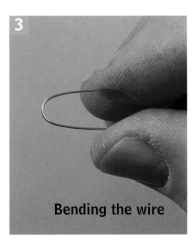

3 Bending the wire

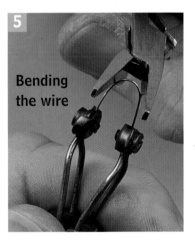

4 Inserting the wire

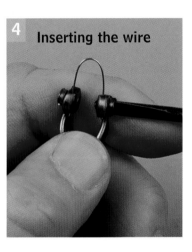

5 Bending the wire

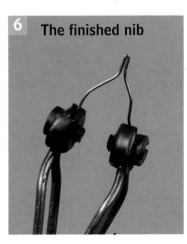

6 The finished nib

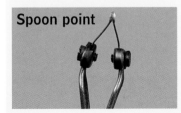

Spoon point

Adding colour

In order to preserve the outline of the pyrography, it is best to use water-soluble paints such as acrylics or gouache. These can be diluted with water without losing colour strength. Water-based felt pens blend well and when the paler colours are used, the various textures of the surface beneath show through the diluted colours.

Water-based crayons

Felt-tipped pen

Permanent felt pens

Acrylic paints

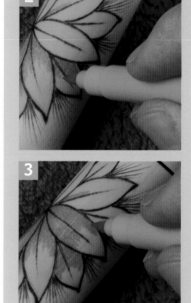

Using water-based felt pens to build up layers of colour

Sketch books

Many artists carry a sketch book with them at all times and ideas can later be developed from any quick sketches. Ideas can come from observing man-made or natural objects. Look out for interesting shapes, textures, colour or patterns. A sketchbook is like a visual diary; it is a resource that you can keep adding to and is always a source of inspiration.

Making marks

Drawing tip

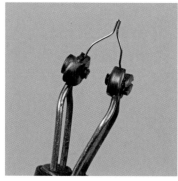
Spoon point

The art of burning requires concentration. The grain of the wood will either assist smooth flow or go against the direction of the tool. By varying the stroke, pressure and heat, it is possible to produce thin and thick lines, deep grooves, dots, textures and tones.

Hold the pyrography pen as you would a pen or pencil, and keep your fingers as near the nib as possible at the bottom of the black plastic sleeve. Do not touch the wire support as it can get very hot. For most woods, the heat control knob should be set so that the wire nib shows just a hint of red. Some woods require a higher heat setting, while veneer and materials like leather, card and hand-made paper need less heat. Too high a setting will cause scorching on either side of your burnt line.

The burning technique is similar to painting or sketching. Work with a smooth movement, starting at the top of the design and working with light, short strokes. Work slowly, to give the wood time to burn. At first, you may get blobs and uneven lines – so keep practising.

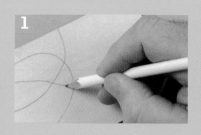
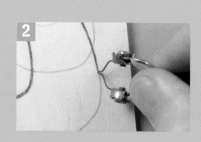
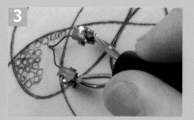

Making a sample board
Take a small rectangle of birch plywood. Using pencil, draw a random line (see right) or draw in a grid pattern. Fill in sections using different techniques.

1 Pencil in a random outline.
2 Burn the outline using a drawing point.
3 Fill in sections to achieve different effects.

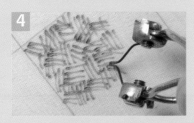

Working effects with a drawing tip

1   Work dots by stippling, just touching the tip to the wood.
2   Work short, straight lines, letting the wire rest for a bit longer at the beginning.
3   Work wavy lines, keeping the pressure on the tip as even as possible.
4   Cross-hatch small sections randomly to produce an interesting effect.
5   Shade diagonally, working a series of fine lines with the pressure on the nib even.
6   Work dense stippling by burning tiny round shapes very closely together.
7   Work freehand circles for a decorative bubble effect.

Working effects with a spoon point

8   Work larger dots, letting the bowl of the spoon point rest on the surface.
9   Work diagonal shading as a series of fine lines.
10 Work spirals with the inverted spoon point.
11 Work diagonal lines slowly to achieve a good burn.
12 Create a random brick effect with different-sized freehand rectangles.

Decorative edges

13 Using a U-shaped nib, on a flat edge.
14 Using a U-shaped nib, on a curved edge.

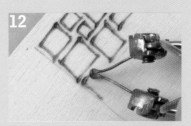

15

Lettering

Good lettering comes with practice. When you try forming these letters, remember to burn them in the direction shown by the arrows. The spoon tip is a good choice for lettering.

Draw out the letters in pencil on ruled lines. If you are unsure, draft out your letters on greaseproof or tracing paper first, to make sure they fit your chosen object. Use masking tape to stick the paper down if necessary. You can then use the paper as a draft to work from.

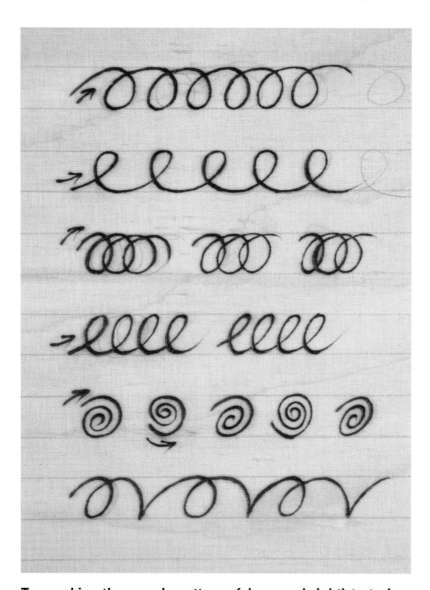

Try working the sample patterns (above and right) to train your hand and eye to produce shapes smoothly.

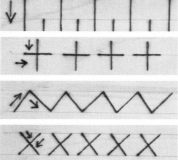

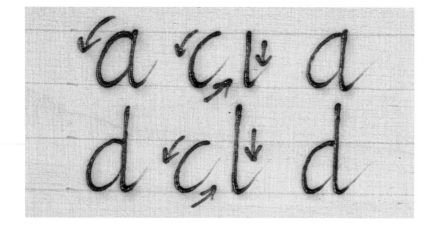

Follow the direction of the arrows on the sample
letters (above and opposite) to work them.

Finishing your work

If left bare, the finished piece can pick up marks and get dirty. For pieces that are to be displayed outdoors, such as house numbers or house name plaques, you need to protect them with yacht varnish. A clear matt or satin varnish can be used for boxes that will be handled regularly. Beeswax is frequently used on finished items, or Danish oil which can be brushed or wiped on and successfully brings out the grain of the wood.

Sanding off any rough edges

Spraying with acrylic gloss varnish

Waxing using a soft cloth

Safety information

Pyrography pen

- Do not touch any part of the hot wire nib with your fingers.

- Hold the pyrography tool as close to the nib as possible but take care not to touch the metal elements. After long periods of working, the elements can become uncomfortably hot. Some models have guards to protect your hands.

- Keep the nib well away from your eyes.

- Make sure children are supervised when using pyrography equipment.

Ventilation

Make sure the room is well ventilated when you are working. Some surfaces, such as old wood, driftwood or leather, can give off nasty fumes. If you have an electric air purifier or a humidifier, use it to remove smoke from the work area.

Dust mask

A dust mask should always be worn when working. This will help to protect against breathing in smoke from the burning wood, or any dust particles produced when you are sanding your work.

Working with fixatives and sealers

- Take care that you do not breathe in fumes when you are working with fixative, spray sealers or varnishes.

- Make sure the room you are working in is well ventilated (see left).

- Wear a dust mask to help prevent you breathing in fumes (see left).

- Always read carefully and follow the instructions given by the manufacturer regarding the use and storage of products.

- Mop up any spills immediately using kitchen paper or rags, and dispose of them carefully.

- Take care to replace the lids of products securely after use.

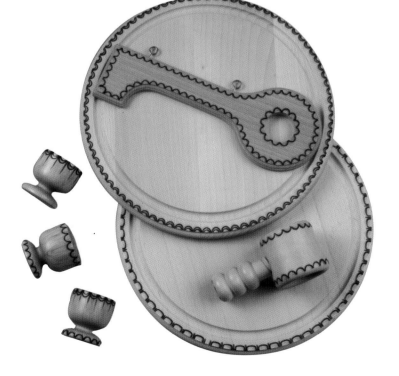

These decorative edges were worked using the method shown on page 15

DOOR NUMBERS

These numbers can be filled in simply or using a variety of patterns. For a different look, fill in the background rather than the number.

You will need...

- Wood blank
- Template
- Drawing tip
- Spoon point
- Pencil

Tip

The number can also be cut out using a small saw (see below).

Design variations using the same template

▼

1 Draw round the template carefully using a pencil.

2 Remove the template to show the outline.

3 Burn the outline of the number using the drawing tip.

4 Stipple in the background of the number using an inverted spoon point.

5 Complete the background, keeping the tone as even as possible.

The blank used

KEYRINGS

These little keyrings are fun and quick to make, and can be personalised to suit people of all ages.

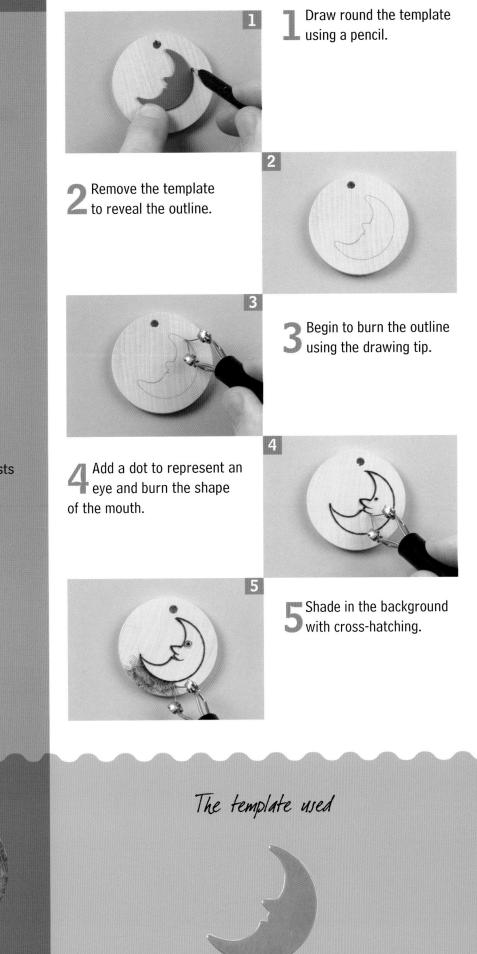

1 Draw round the template using a pencil.

2 Remove the template to reveal the outline.

3 Begin to burn the outline using the drawing tip.

4 Add a dot to represent an eye and burn the shape of the mouth.

5 Shade in the background with cross-hatching.

You will need...

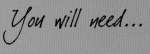

- Keyring blank
- Template
- Drawing tip
- Pencil

Tip

Choose the design on the keyring to suit the interests of the recipient.

The completed design

The template used

COASTERS

Coasters are always useful, and you can make a matching set with just one pattern or a set that uses lots of different ones.

You will need...

- Wood blank
- Rubber stamp
- Ink pad
- Drawing tip

Tip

Do not overload the rubber stamp with ink. Stamp the first print on to scrap paper, as excess ink on the wood can cause bleeding.

The completed design

▼

1 Press the stamp firmly on the pad to ink it.

2 Stamp the design on the centre of the coaster.

3 Burn the outline of the design using the drawing tip.

4 Still using the drawing tip, use stippling and stroking techniques to fill in the dark areas.

5 Cross-hatch the background.

The rubber stamp used

SPOONS

These spoons are inexpensive to buy, make lovely gifts or bazaar items, and are an ideal project for the beginner.

1 Draw the design on the spoon freehand, using a towel to support it.

2 Still using the towel for support, begin to burn the outline of the design.

3 Complete the outline using a simple line.

4 Begin to add the fine detail to the design.

5 Complete the effect by adding lines that radiate from the outline.

You will need...

- Wood blank
- Drawing tip
- Pencil
- Eraser
- Rolled towel

Tip

Choose a spoon with a wide, flat rim when working a patterned edge.

The completed design
▼

The drawing used

PENCIL BOX

The design used for this box is based on a favourite stencil, but a completely freehand design would be equally suitable.

You will need...

- Pencil box blank
- Copper template
- Pencil
- Eraser
- Drawing tip
- Permanent marker pens (optional)

Tip

Make sure you leave enough space in the design to add a name.

The completed design, before the addition of colour

▼

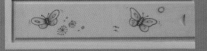

1 Place the butterfly template on the box and draw round it using a sharp pencil.

2 Draw the rest of the design freehand.

3 Burn the outlines using a drawing tip.

4 Colour in the design if desired, using permanent marker pens.

The templates used

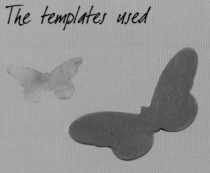

PENCIL BLOCK

Children love these useful pencil blocks, and anything that helps youngsters to be tidy is always useful!

1 Stamp the motif on the blank, making sure it is correctly placed.

2 Using the towel for support, burn the outline of the figure.

3 Draw in the goal and pitch freehand, using a sharp pencil.

4 Complete the outline.

5 Colour in the design if required using permanent marker pens.

You will need...

- Pencil block blank
- Rubber stamp
- Ink pad
- Pencil
- Drawing tip
- Rolled towel
- Permanent marker pens (optional)

Tips

A name or message can be added to the other side.

The completed item before the addition of colour

The rubber stamp used

LETTER RACK

This quickly-worked item is a great way to tidy up those piles of letters that seem to accumulate all over the house.

1 Layer the carbon paper and the design and fix both to the blank using masking tape.

You will need...

- Wood blank
- Design to fit the front of the rack
- Carbon paper
- Ballpoint pen
- Drawing tip
- Masking tape
- Rolled towel

Tip

You could use someone's name or the word LETTERS as the main design on this.

The completed item

▼

2 Draw round the design, using a ballpoint pen and pressing firmly.

3 Peel the carbon back carefully, making sure all the design has transferred.

4 Burn in the outline of the design.

5 Complete the shading.

The drawing used

COATHANGER

Pyrography is a great way to turn a basic household item into something that is beautiful as well as useful.

You will need...

- Plain wood coathanger
- Design to fit the front of the coathanger
- Carbon paper
- Ballpoint pen
- Drawing tip
- Masking tape

Tip

Use a nursery motif and add a child's name to a hanger to encourage tidiness.

The completed coathanger

▼

1 Layer the carbon paper and the design and fix to the coathanger using masking tape.

2 Draw the design using a ballpoint pen and pressing firmly.

3 Peel the carbon back carefully, making sure the design has transferred.

4 Burn in the design.

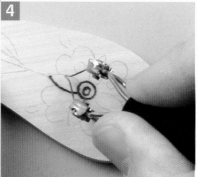

The drawing used

HANGING NOTEPAD

This is a great way to make sure you always have paper handy. Pads are easily replaced and attached using double-sided adhesive pads.

You will need...

- Wood blank
- Design to fit the front of the blank
- Carbon paper
- Ballpoint pen
- Drawing tip
- Masking tape
- Double-sided adhesive pads

Tip

Keep a pad by the telephone for messages and another in the kitchen for shopping lists.

The completed design

▼

1 Layer the carbon paper and the design and fix to the blank using masking tape.

2 Draw the design using a ballpoint pen and pressing firmly.

3 Peel the carbon back carefully, making sure all the design has transferred.

4 Burn in the outline of the design.

5 Complete the shading.

6 Attach the notepad using double-sided adhesive pads.

The drawing used

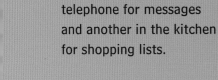

CORKSCREW

How many times have you searched through a drawer to find a corkscrew? The answer may be to make one that is so attractive it can be left out all the time!

You will need...

- Plain wooden corkscrew
- Design to fit the front of the corkscrew
- Carbon paper
- Ballpoint pen
- Drawing tip
- Masking tape
- Rolled towel

Tip

Burn the relevant name and date for a special birthday or wedding gift.

The completed design

▼

1 Layer the carbon paper and the design and fix to the blank using masking tape.

2 Draw over the design using a ballpoint pen and pressing down firmly.

3 Peel the carbon back carefully, making sure all the design has transferred.

4 Burn in the outline of the design.

5 Complete the shading.

The drawing used

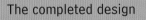

PICTURE FRAME

An interesting pattern can be produced by drawing lots of little circles all over an item – try it and see.

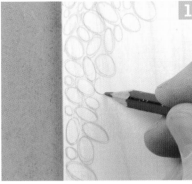

1 Using a sharp pencil, draw random circles all over the frame.

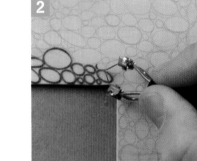

2 Using the drawing tip, burn in each individual circle.

You will need...

- Plain wood frame
- Pencil
- Drawing tip

Tip

This design could also be used as the frame for a mirror.

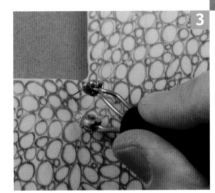

3 Complete the design, making sure the whole frame is covered.

The completed frame

▼

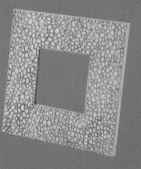

Detail of the pattern used

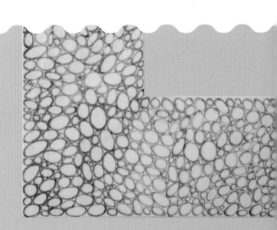

JEWELLERY BOX

This pretty box is just right for keeping small trinkets safely, and can be worked to match any colour scheme.

You will need...

- Plain wooden box
- Design to fit lid
- Carbon paper
- Ballpoint pen
- Drawing tip
- Masking tape
- Permanent marker pens
- Masking tape
- Rolled towel

Tip

Line the box with felt and add a message to the inside of the lid.

The completed box

▼

1 Fix the carbon and the pattern to the top of the box using masking tape.

2 Draw over firmly using a ballpoint pen.

3 Peel back the design, making sure it has transferred.

4 Begin to burn the outline using the drawing tip.

5 Colour in the design if desired using permanent marker pens.

The drawing used

MIRROR

Many different patterns can be used for frames,
depending on the subject. This one is a favourite.

You will need...

- Plain wood mirror
- Design to fit edge of mirror
- Carbon paper
- Ballpoint pen
- Drawing tip
- Masking tape

Tips

If you want to make a mirror for a child, replace the mirror with mirrored perspex.

The completed mirror frame

▼

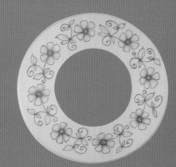

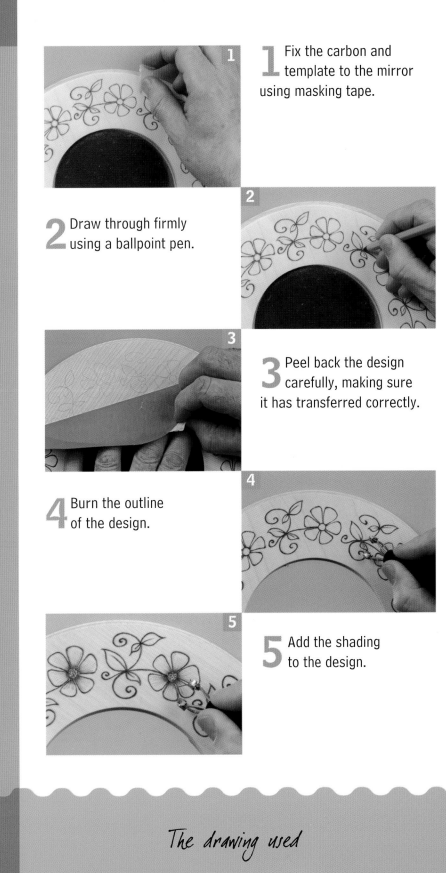

1 Fix the carbon and template to the mirror using masking tape.

2 Draw through firmly using a ballpoint pen.

3 Peel back the design carefully, making sure it has transferred correctly.

4 Burn the outline of the design.

5 Add the shading to the design.

The drawing used

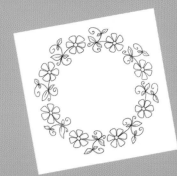

TINY BOX

This little box would be the perfect way to present a tiny, precious gift like a ring, a charm bracelet or a locket.

1 Fix the carbon and the design to the box using masking tape.

2 Using a towel to support your hand, draw over the design with the ballpoint pen.

3 Peel back the carbon paper carefully to make sure the design has transferred properly.

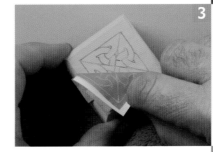

4 Burn the outline.

5 Add the shading.

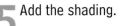

You will need...

- Plain wooden box with lid
- Design to fit lid of box
- Carbon paper
- Drawing tip
- Lining material (optional)
- Masking tape
- Rolled towel

Tip

You could burn the other surfaces of this small box and then line it with felt.

The completed box

▼

The drawing used

BUTTERFLY BOWL

The design on this bowl is a favourite motif, and it can be coloured
using felt-tip pens for a brighter effect.

You will need...

- Small turned bowl
- Butterfly template to fit rim
- Pencil
- Drawing tip
- Felt-tip pens
- Masking tape
- Rolled towel

Tip

Use a centre finder, (available from Craft Supplies Ltd., see list on page 80) to plot the radiating lines accurately.

The finished bowl

▼

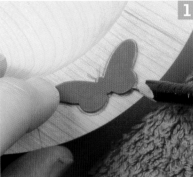

1 Pencil in radiating lines. Place the template on the edge of the bowl and draw round it with a pencil.

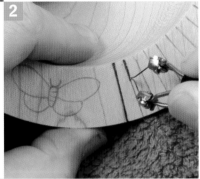

2 Burn the radiating lines using the drawing tip, using the rolled towel to support your wrist.

3 Still using the drawing tip, burn the outline of the butterfly.

4 Add the finer detail to the inner rim of the bowl.

The template used

49

WOODGRAIN BOWL

The decoration on this bowl varies according to the grain of the wood,
which means that each one is absolutely unique.

You will need...

- Small turned wooden bowl
- Pencil
- Drawing tip
- Spoon point
- Rolled towel

Tip

Select a bowl that has plenty of interesting grain pattern for this project.

The completed bowl

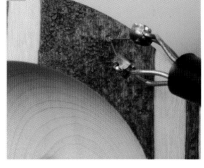

1 Look carefully at the bowl to decide which areas to highlight.

2 Using a pencil, pick out the highlights of the grain and burn them in using the drawing tip.

3 Using the towel to support your arm as you work, fill in the detail.

4 Block in the larger areas using the spoon point.

Design ideas

Types of wood burn differently and the grain pattern varies, so you can produce a range of effects. You could also add colour or a coloured varnish to the finished bowl.

BREAD BOARD

This is a perfect example of an item that can be both useful and beautiful. The design of ears of wheat is ideal.

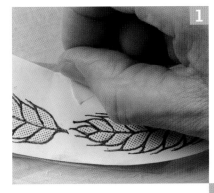

1 Layer the carbon paper and the design and fix to the edge of the board using masking tape.

2 Remove carbon. Draw the design using a ballpoint pen and pressing firmly.

3 Using a towel to support your arm, burn in the outline of the design.

4 Complete the shading of the ears of wheat.

You will need...

- Plain wooden board
- Design to fit the surface of the board
- Carbon paper
- Ballpoint pen
- Drawing tip
- Masking tape
- Rolled towel

Tip

For use with food, coat the board with pure sunflower oil, Tung oil or Danish oil.

The completed design
▼

The drawing used

CANDLEHOLDER

This pretty holder contains an ordinary household night-light, and the simple design echoes the shapes of candle flames.

1 Draw the design in pencil, using the drawing below for reference. Use a towel to support your wrist.

You will need...

- Plain wood night-light holder
- Pencil
- Eraser
- Drawing tip
- Felt-tip pens
- Rolled towel

Tip

As with all candles, never leave this one burning unattended.

2 Using a towel for support, begin to burn the design.

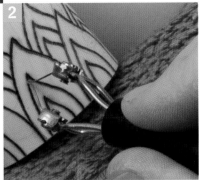

3 Add shading.

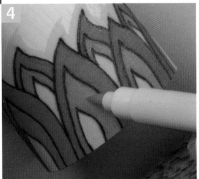

4 Add colour using felt-tip pens.

The completed candleholder

▼

The drawing used

CELTIC BOX

Celtic designs are always popular, and using a rubber stamp is a quick,
easy way to reproduce the intricacy of the pattern.

1 Layer the photocopied design and carbon on the lid of the box and fix down with masking tape.

2 Using the towel for support, draw through the design firmly using a ballpoint pen.

You will need...

- Small wooden box
- Rubber stamp
- Ink pad
- Photocopier paper
- Pencil
- Drawing tip
- Rolled towel
- Ballpoint pen
- Carbon paper

Tip

Enlarge or reduce the image on a photocopier to fit the size of your box, then transfer using carbon paper.

3 Peel back the carbon, making sure the design has transferred.

4 Burn the design.

5 Complete the shading.

The completed box
▼

The rubber stamp used

CHEESEBOARD

The cheeky mouse in this design is endlessly popular, but you can use a different design if you prefer.

1 Layer the carbon paper and the design and fix to the blank using masking tape.

You will need...

- Plain wooden cheeseboard
- Design to fit the front of the board
- Carbon paper
- Ballpoint pen
- Drawing tip
- Masking tape

2 Draw the design through using a ballpoint pen.

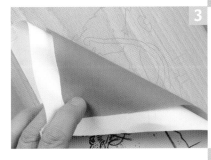

3 Peel back the design carefully, making sure it has transferred.

Tip

For use with food, coat the board with pure sunflower oil, tung oil or Danish oil.

4 Burn the outline of the little mouse.

5 Complete the shading.

The completed cheeseboard

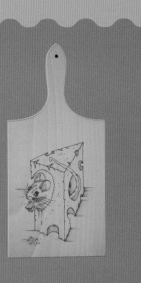

The drawing used

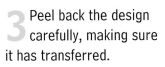

CANDLESTICK

The shape of the base of this candlestick meant that it was easier to draw the design freehand, using a sketch as inspiration, to follow the shape of the base.

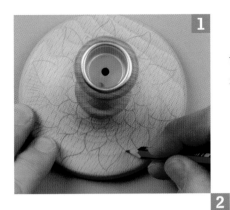

1 Draw the design on to the base of the candlestick using a sharp pencil.

2 Burn in the 'flame' shapes using the drawing tip.

3 Add the detail.

You will need...

- Plain wooden candlestick
- Pencil
- Eraser
- Drawing tip

Tip

Make sure you never leave an unattended candle burning.

Detail of the completed candlestick

▼

The drawing used

CAMEO BOX

With a suitable inscription added to the inside of the lid, this very feminine trinket box would make an ideal birthday or bridesmaid's gift.

1 Fix the design and carbon paper to the box lid with masking tape and draw over with ballpoint pen.

2 Remove carefully, making sure all the design has transferred.

3 Using a towel for support, begin to burn in the outlines.

4 Begin to build up the shading.

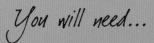

You will need...

- Plain wood box
- Design
- Carbon paper
- Ballpoint pen
- Drawing tip
- Masking tape
- Rolled towel

Tip

A head design also looks very effective in silhouette, worked using a spoon point.

5 Complete the detail.

The drawing used

The completed box

NAPKIN RINGS

Napkin rings are always useful. Why not make a different design for each member of the family?

1 Draw the freehand design on the napkin ring using a pencil.

2 Draw round the template, holding it in place with your thumb.

3 Using a rolled towel to support your hand, begin to burn the outline using a drawing tip.

4 Build up the detail on the butterfly.

5 Complete the shading.

You will need...

- Plain wooden rings
- Templates or designs
- Pencil
- Drawing tip
- Masking tape
- Rolled towel

Tip

Personalise these napkin rings for dinner guests, and let them take them home with them as a reminder of a special occasion.

A completed napkin ring

▼

Design ideas

The decoration I used was stencilled and drawn freehand, but you can ring the changes by using rubber stamps or just lettering.

65

CANDY BOX

Both the top and the base of this cute little box have been decorated with designs worked freehand from sketches.

You will need...

- Circular wooden box
- Pencil
- Eraser
- Drawing tip
- Rolled towel

Tip

This box could also be used for jewellery, pot-pourri or even loose change.

The completed box and lid

▼

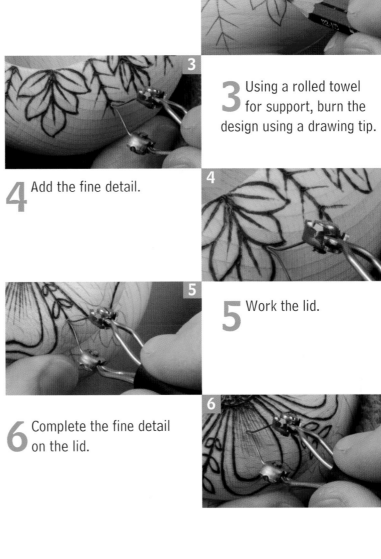

1 Draw the design on the lid of the box freehand using a pencil.

2 Draw a similar design on the base of the box.

3 Using a rolled towel for support, burn the design using a drawing tip.

4 Add the fine detail.

5 Work the lid.

6 Complete the fine detail on the lid.

The drawings used

LEATHER COIN PURSES

These little purses are inexpensive to buy, quick to work and are always useful, so they make the perfect little gift!

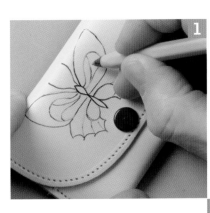

1 Draw the design on the purse using the template and a ballpoint pen.

You will need...

- Plain leather purse
- Ballpoint pen/pencil
- Drawing tip
- Permanent marker pens (optional)

Tip

Leather is very easy to work, but it is best to draw the design using a ballpoint pen or a pencil.

2 Burn the outline using a drawing tip.

3 Colour in parts of the design if desired using permanent marker pens.

The completed coin purse

The drawing used

MONEY BOX

This psychedelic money box looks like a giant toadstool, and the bright colours would appeal to a small child.

You will need...

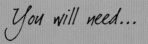

- Money box blank
- Pencil
- Eraser
- Drawing tip
- Acrylic paints
- Paint brush
- Rolled towel
- Varnish

Tips

The colours for this design can be chosen to match a child's bedroom or playroom.

The completed box

1 Draw the design freehand on the lid, using the drawing as a guide.

2 Draw the design freehand on the body of the 'toadstool'.

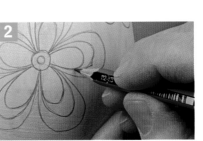

3 Using the towel for support, begin to burn the design.

4 Complete the design.

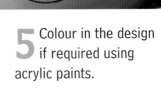

5 Colour in the design if required using acrylic paints.

6 Finish colouring the design. When it's dry seal the colours with varnish.

The drawing used

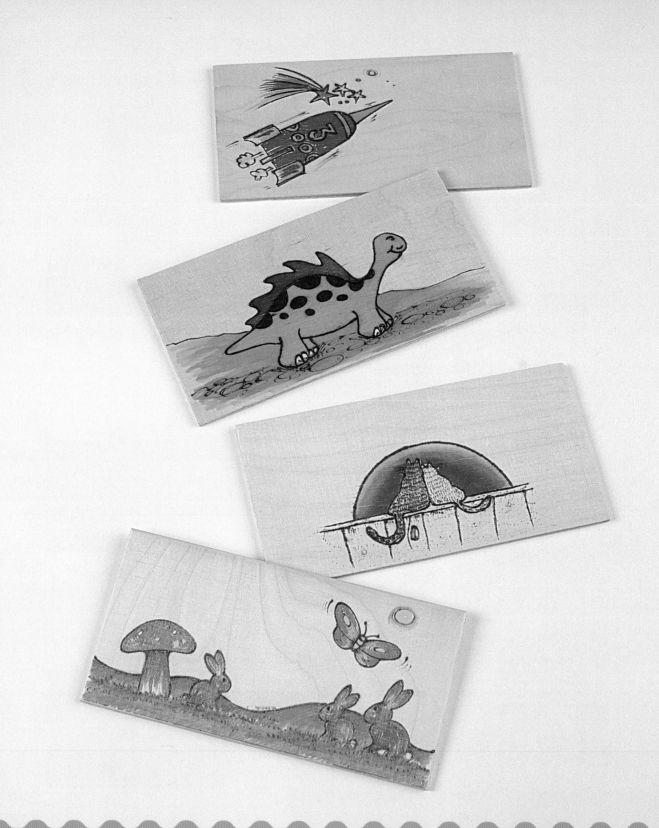

DOOR PLAQUES

Children love to label their rooms, and these simply-worked plaques have a space left for a name.

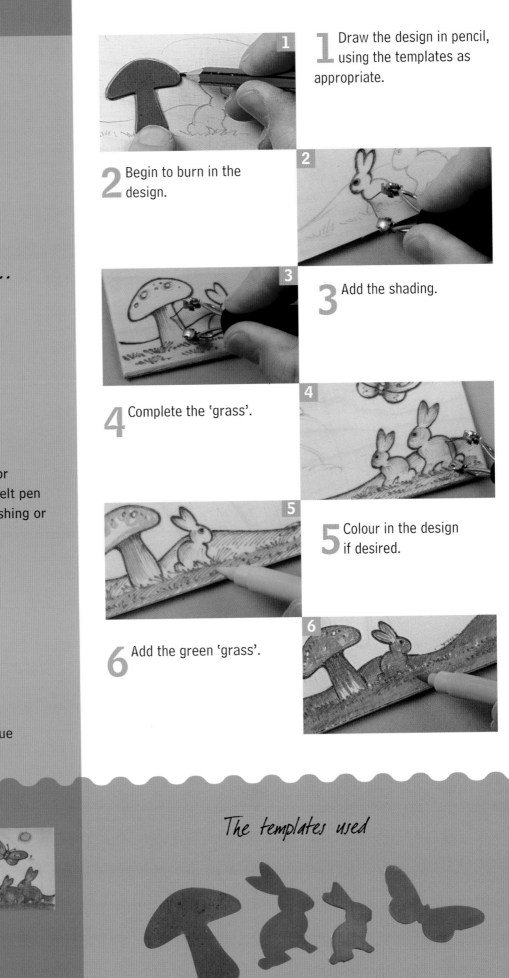

1 Draw the design in pencil, using the templates as appropriate.

2 Begin to burn in the design.

3 Add the shading.

4 Complete the 'grass'.

5 Colour in the design if desired.

6 Add the green 'grass'.

You will need...

- Wooden blanks
- Copper templates
- Drawing tip
- Felt pens

Tip

Use artists' fixative or hairspray to fix the felt pen colours before varnishing or sealing.

The completed plaque

▼

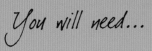

The templates used

NEEDLECASES

These neat little containers help to keep needles safely in one place, and should delight any keen needleworker you know.

You will need...

- Plain turned needlecase
- Pencil
- Eraser
- Drawing tip
- Permanent marker pens

Tips

If you want to colour your design make sure you use a permanent marker pen, as it will get a lot of wear.

The completed design

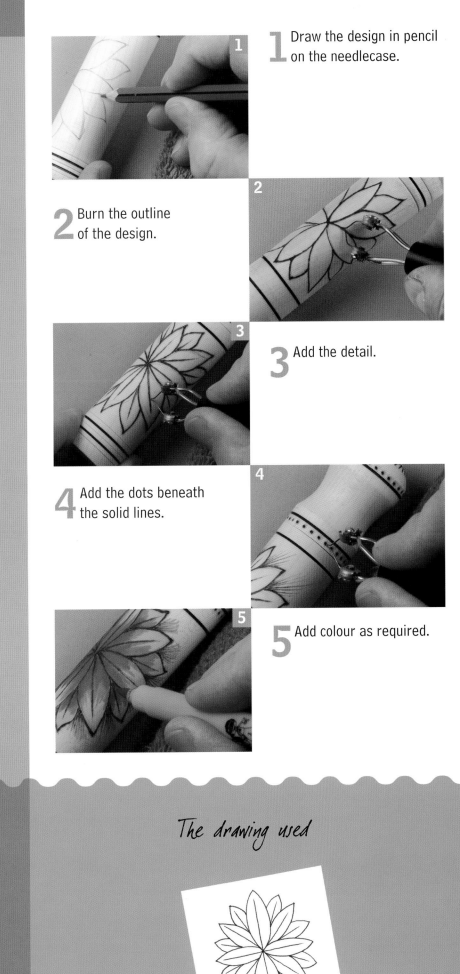

1 Draw the design in pencil on the needlecase.

2 Burn the outline of the design.

3 Add the detail.

4 Add the dots beneath the solid lines.

5 Add colour as required.

The drawing used

KEY RACK

Every home has lots of different keys to look after, and this handy rack
is an attractive way to keep them organised.

You will need...

- Wood blank
- Design to fit the front of the blank
- Carbon paper
- Ballpoint pen
- Drawing tip
- Masking tape
- Acrylic paint
- Brush
- Varnish

Tip

With a name and date added, this would make an ideal 18th or 21st birthday present.

Detail of completed design

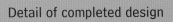

1 Layer the carbon paper and the design and fix using masking tape.

2 Transfer the design using a ballpoint pen and pressing firmly.

3 Peel the carbon back carefully, making sure all the design has transferred.

4 Burn in the outline of the design.

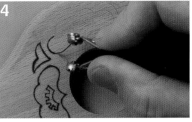

5 Complete the shading.

6 Add colour if desired using acrylic paint. When it's dry seal with varnish.

The drawing used

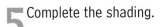

VENEER GREETINGS CARD

Burning a design on a piece of veneer makes an attractive panel
for the front of a greetings card.

You will need...

- Card blank
- Small piece of veneer
- Pencil
- Felt pens
- Adhesive stick

Tip

Burr maple, masur birch and bird's eye maple have interesting grain features that would work well as background for the main design. Coloured veneers are also good for this project.

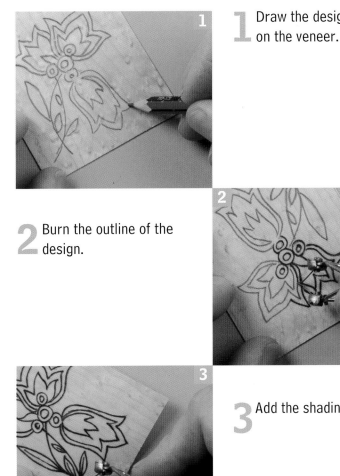

1 Draw the design on the veneer.

2 Burn the outline of the design.

3 Add the shading.

4 Colour and mount on the card.

The completed card

▼

The drawing used

USEFUL ADDRESSES

Acrylics and finishes
Westcountry Finishes
Unit 4, Station Business Park
Lower Brimley Ind. Estate
Teignmouth, Devon
TQ14 8QJ/01626 779994
email:westcountryfinishes
@virgin.net

Blanks, boxes, veneers, transfer paper, finishes
Craft Supplies Ltd.
The Mill, Miller's Dale
Nr Buxton, Derbyshire
SK17 8SN /01298 871636
www.craft-supplies.co.uk

Blanks, cut-out service
Humble Bee, The Oaklands
Stroat, Chepstow
NP16 7LR / 01594 529237

Copper templates
Milton Bridge, Unit 9, Trent
Trading Park, Botteslow St.,
Stoke-on-Trent
ST1 3NA / 01782 274229

Fred Aldous
Dept. CN, 37 Lever St
Manchester
M1 1LW / 8707 517302
www.fredaldous.co.uk

Leather products
Nicola Cheyette, 55 Pine Tree
Ave., Leicester
LE5 1AL / 01162 768056

Spray finishes
Chestnut Products,
PO Box 536, Ipswich, Suffolk
IPN 5WN / 01473 425878

Pyrography machines
Peter Child Woodturning
The Old Hyde, Little Yeldham
Near Halstead, Essex
CO9 4QT / 01787 237291

Rubber stamps
Imagina, Ludwells Farm,
Spode Lane, Cowden, Kent
TN8 7HN / 01342 850111

Turned bowls
Alan Truman, 14 Chestnut
Avenue, Kirkby in Ashfield
Nottinghamshire
NG17 8BB / 01623 754893

INDEX